MW01317276

This book made available in part by a generous gift from the Dale Hull memorial fund thru the Lomax Church of Christ.

BIBLICAL KEYS TO EFFECTIVE MINISTRY

ISBN: 9798361719327

Published by The Jenkins Institute

thejenkinsinstitute.com

Editing: Jennifer Hammit
Cover Logo: Andrew Jenkins
Interior layout: Joey Sparks

JEFF & DALE JENKINS

Dale here:
Obviously Jeff does not know about this. That'd be odd for the guy who co-wrote a book to dedicate it to himself. But if the book is on ministry, I dedicate this book to my older brother, Jeff. He, in every aspect of his life, is a minister. He is the best preacher I know, but he is the rarest of men who is equally effective as both preacher and minister. Both in his intimate life within the congregations he has served as well as his broader life with old friends, members of congregations he has preached at in the past, those he has visited, and especially with his fellow ministers, his counsel is sought and his wisdom is wanted because of his tremendous heart for others. He has since college been the minister I have looked toward to go before me and show me the way. And with a four-year (he says three) head start, I know that what he has faced is coming and he has ever been my earthly model on how to handle what's next.
Thank you, Jeff. I love you.

THE KEYS

1. If God's Word is not your Northern Light, you may be many things, but you will never be truly effective.
2. "Has the Word of God spoken to this matter?"
3. You must be a Christian.
4. You need some others (a Paul, a Barnabas, and a Timothy) in your life.
5. Keep growing and keep improving.
6. Is there evidence in your ministry that the fruit born of the Spirit is growing in your life?
7. Jesus really is the answer to every struggle in our lives and every problem in our world.
8. Never give up on people!
9. Your outlook and attitude affect your effectiveness.
10. Work hard and to love your work.
11. Always believe you got the better end of the bargain.

12. Let the elders be the elders.
13. Enjoy the team you have and work toward building it.
14. Influence is cash.
15. Don't look.
16. There is no true peace without God.
17. There is a direct correlation between how quickly you get over a hurt and the effectiveness of your ministry.
18. You can't just talk about faith. To be effective you have to be living it out.
19. Sometimes you have to not get your way and be joyful about it.
20. The vocal negative minority will always be around. We can and should hear their hearts, but we must not allow them to prevail.
21. Just keep going.
22. Do some things just because you are a Christian.
23. We can't do it all, but we can all do something.
24. "Preach the word and love the people!"
25. Remember we are all very much alike.

But watch thou in all things, endure afflictions, do the work of an evangelist, make full proof of thy ministry.

2 Timothy 4:5

King James Version

INTRODUCTION

Your opportunity to stay in ministry and be effective is in direct proportion to several significant attitudes and actions. I am sure this list is not exhaustive but does reflect what I have observed. In writing this book I am not setting myself up as any sort of expert in ministry. In fact quite the opposite. Much of what I share here are lessons I've learned from my own mistakes. Every time I have felt like I had this thing called ministry figured out some unexpected curve ball would come my way.

After 40+ years of local ministry I wanted to put a few things on paper that I have observed and experienced that have helped me and others to any degree of effectiveness. I am writing from the most humbled of standpoints. I do not fain that I am good at this. I've been a student since day one. But I have long studied the art of ministering well, in fact, all I've ever wanted to be was a preacher (I even wrote another book by that title).

Whether you are reading this hoping for some insight, or are old and experienced, perhaps you'll nod and agree or you might offer differing advice. Regardless, I am thankful for you and pray God blesses your service to Him.

Ministry carries its own unique challenges and joys. You can, and probably will go in the same day to visit a family who has welcomed a new soul into the world, another family who is keeping vigil as another soul bursts through to its eternal reward, and yet another family who is celebrating a new soul added to God's Family, redeemed from sin. Where else can an audience all hear one message and some are moved to change their whole life, others are angered to the point of profanity, and others are indifferent? Where else do you get to be closer to the throne of heaven but have to go, as if, one-on-one with satan's minions.

There's probably not a thing in here entirely original with us. So many have poured into our lives, from parents to other family members, to mentor ministers, contemporary preachers, and younger heroes, from our children, to our shepherds. We owe them all and if this book should aid any of you reading each would say that was enough for them. For now, thank you. And while we're saying thanks, thanks to our expert proofing person, Jennifer. And to our dear friend and our format guy at TJI, Jo(e)y Sparks. We are blessed men. —*dj*

As for you, always be sober-minded, endure suffering, do the work of an evangelist, fulfill your ministry.

2 Timothy 4:5

English Standard Version

THE WORD OF GOD AS YOUR NORTH STAR

There are going to be some people who will try to steer you in sorts of directions. Sources, resources, and advice will certainly be needed for you to be effective in ministry. But for a 100 generations, THE GO-TO SOURCE has been—and should the Lord tarry for 100 generations more, it will be the Word of God.

The prophet Isaiah over 2500 years ago had some insight into this: "The grass withers, the flower fades, but the word of our God will stand forever" (Isaiah 40:8).

That same Word is the source of true faith in any true believer. "So faith comes from hearing, and hearing through the word of Christ" (Romans 10:17). **In your own personal devotion to Christ and in your min-**

istry in Christ, if His Word is not your Northern Light you may be many things, but you will never be truly effective. We have often seen men rocket off in popularity who have rested their ministry on their winsome personality, their ability to turn a phrase or to bring a laugh. If your ministry is built on those things you will either flame out or eventually lead people astray.

There seems to have been a shift among many ministers today. The desire to connect, relate, and fit in has moved some ministers from the Text. We must believe and embrace that truth is truth! Error is also error. —*dj*

You, however, be self-controlled in all things,
endure hardship, do an evangelist's work,
fulfill your ministry.

2 Timothy 4:5

New English Translation (NET Bible)

THE FIRST QUESTION

Most people who use the word "liberalism" do not know what it means. Classical liberalism is a denial of the inspiration of the scriptures.

To remain effective you must have the mentality that says: "Everything else may be wrong, but the Bible is right." Every key in this book finds its foundation in that truth. Here's the first and most significant of our keys: **The first and most important question is, "Has the Word of God spoken to this matter?"** And if it has, it sets our boundaries.

Without this key, you may appear to be successful, effective, and even beloved. You may be highly sought after for your knowledge. You may be followed by many for your abilities. You may be admired for your creativity. BUT you will not be pleasing to God.

I suggest you guard what you take in about the Word of God. And if we continually fill our minds with error we will be influenced by it. “Do not be deceived: “Bad company ruins good morals”(1 Corinthians 15:33). Notice we are warned to not be deceived, which certainly implies that it might be easy to be deceived. You may believe yourself strong enough to overcome the influence of those who do not respect God’s Word, but you also may be deceived. You may believe you are OK and even become entrenched in a relationship when someone warns you or questions you on it, but you may be deceived. And in the end, if you surround your life with the teachings, writings, and influences that do not love the Word of God—and it is the Word of God—then you are subjecting yourself to ruin.

Yet, this book is not about the negative, but the positive. With God’s Word as your shelter, with His Inspired Truth as your North Star, with His revealed breath as your compass, you will become more and more effective throughout your ministry. —*dj*

But you, keep your head in all situations, endure hardship, do the work of an evangelist, discharge all the duties of your ministry.

2 Timothy 4:5

New International Version

FIRST THINGS FIRST

It may be cliche but if you really want to be effective in this thing called ministry you have to put first things first.

The first thing must be that you are a Christian. You want to minister, you want to impact lives, you want to do great things in the Lord's Vineyard, BUT before all of those things, and in all of those things, and after all of those things, you are first and foremost a Christian.

Our friend, Matthew Morine, wrote it this way: "Yesterday I spoke at the Bear Valley School of Preaching about three pieces of advice for ministers. The first piece of advice I believe to be most important. It was 'pursue knowing God rather than pursuing how to be good at ministry.'"

Without this we are just professionals striving to be at the top in our field. Without the passionate pursuit of knowing Jesus and being like Him, we might work hard and grow our reputation, but we are empty of any true eternal value or reward.

We become like the Pharisees, we "have our reward already"(Matt. 6:1-6). Those of us striving for excellence in ministry would do well to re-read those words front the Lord and let them sink into our soul and challenge our motives.

Paul, who certainly is a gold standard of effectiveness, worded his pursuit clearly in Philippians 3, "whatever gain I had, I counted as loss for the sake of Christ. Indeed, I count everything as loss because of the surpassing worth of knowing Christ Jesus my Lord. For his sake I have suffered the loss of all things and count them as rubbish, in order that I may gain Christ and be found in him, not having a righteousness of my own that comes from the law, but that which comes through faith in Christ, the righteousness from God that depends on faith—

that I may know him and the power of his resurrection, and may share his sufferings, becoming like him in his death..." (vss. 7-10).

Psalm 46 instructs us, "Stop *striving* and know that I am God;" (vs. 10). As you plan your day the night before you go to bed or when you wake up in the morning, pray over that never-ending to-do list. Stop striving in vain to promote yourself. Instead work toward godly tasks as God's errand boy. Your day belongs to Him - first things first! —*dj*

But you be alert in all things. Suffer wicked treatment. Do the work of an evangelist. Fulfill your ministry.

2 Timothy 4:5

The Everlasting Gospel (Hugo McCord)

GET SOME GUYS

John Donne said: "No man is an island entirely of itself."

Clarence said: "Remember, George: No man is a failure who has friends."

The wisest man who'd ever lived said: "Two are better than one, because they have a good reward for their toil. For if they fall, one will lift up his fellow. But woe to him who is alone when he falls and has not another to lift him up! Again, if two lie together, they keep warm, but how can one keep warm alone? And though a man might prevail against one who is alone, two will withstand him- a threefold cord is not quickly broken"(Ecclesiastes 4:9-12).

Of course, God said it best: "It is not good for man to be alone" (Genesis 2:18).

The simple fact is to be most effective in life you need some others in your life.

In fact there are three people every minister needs in their life:

1. Every minister needs a Paul in their life: Someone older and experienced who has been there before. We need someone who has lived for the Lord and can tell us the effort is worth it. We need someone who has failed, is aware of it, but has continued to serve well.

2. Every minister needs a Barnabas in their life: We need someone with whom we can enjoy life. We all need people who are our age and at the same point we are in our ministry that we can discuss challenges, opportunities, and realities of that ministry with. We need people who are close enough to us to speak hard truths in our lives because of the time and energy invested in those relationships.

3. Every minister needs a Timothy in their life: We need some who we are encouraging to continue. Some who will give us hope for the future. Someone in whom we can invest the lessons of our lives in hopes they will be better than we have been.

As you collect these people, especially those who will influence you while you are young in your ministry, be careful that you select spiritual mentors who are trustworthy and who are true to the Lord. Be careful that you pick people who love the Lord and His Church. Remember it was the Lord Himself who warned that false teachers are "wolves come in sheep's clothing." —*jj*

But you should control yourself at all times, accept troubles, do the work of telling the Good News, and complete all the duties of a servant of God.

2 Timothy 4:5

New Century Version

DON'T STOP GROWING & IMPROVING

Here is how it happens with many of us: We start preaching and the little old ladies of the church tell us how good we are. Bless these gracious souls. Listen to them and love them.They do so much in encouraging young men to go into preaching and ministry. But don't let them convince you that you are the greatest preacher ever.

Over time we begin to learn what works with an audience and what does not. It rarely affects (and should not) our doctrine/ beliefs, but for many ministers, it does affect their presentation. That's where human nature takes over for some of us. We unconsciously develop a pattern and we follow that pattern because it works for us. And we stick with it.

Because preaching doesn't require continuing education hours and because there are minimal opportunities out there to train us to be better at delivering our messages; and because it is not the excellencies of ourselves but of God we are promoting, our presentations become stagnant. We don't learn to advance in our abilities, we don't change our style, and we don't study to be better at "the art of preaching."

You've probably heard, as I have, that "if you don't grow, you die." The earliest advice I remember from heroes of the faith when I was younger was about continuing to study and grow. Time has proven that those who gave that advice were right. The hard work of study and preparing, the delight of discovery and design, the charm of constructing and composing pay off. You cannot coast. It will show. You'll succumb to proof-texting, you'll pull text out of context, you'll develop a handful of "fall back on" texts and not deliver the breadth and depth of the Scriptures. You'll just fill the time and the air with words. And, you'll be boring and probably won't know why.

But this is also true for your presentation skills. If you do not keep improving on them, honing them, and studying them you'll grow more predictable. Your patterns will cause the audience to check out, you'll find yourself monotone, and, to put it frankly, you won't be interesting to listen to. So, many people will not. You'll blame it on their lack of interest in spiritual things, and you may be right, but even the best food is better with a little seasoning.

If you want to be most effective in your preaching you will work hardest on the text and dredging it for the riches therein, but you will also give attention to improving your presentation skills. A few quick things that have helped others:

1. Study great speakers: Watch their style, their eyes, their hands, and their movements. Listen to their syntax, their voice inflections, and the words they weave together. You don't want to become scripted but ob-

serve and learn. I am not just talking about effective preachers, but also other effective speakers. Listen to product launchers on YouTube. Google "greatest speeches of all time." You aren't getting theology from these folks but tips on style.

2. Read books on presenting: *Speak with No Fear,* Carnegie's *How to Win Friends and Influence People,* Pollard's *The Compelling Communicator, 100 Things Every Presenter Needs to Know About People* by Weinschenik, *How to Deliver A TED Talk.* That should get you started.

3. Get others to grade you (if you dare): Ask some people who you know love you and want the best for you to help you recognize irritating things about you when you speak. I learned that I lower my voice too much when I am making a sensitive point. If you can't handle hearing the feedback, don't ask them.

4. Get someone to critique you professionally: You are probably aware that most executives and politicians have coaches. Well, what we are doing is exponentially

more significant than what they are doing. You can share some links with a professional stage coach or have them come and review you in person. I learned that I tend to "move without purpose." And have worked to make my movements on stage movements with purpose.

The primary point in all of this is that to be the most effective, you want to be the best at every part of your work. **So keep growing and keep improving.** —*dj*

But you, be sober in all things, endure hardship, do the work of an evangelist, fulfill your ministry.

2 Timothy 4:5

New American Standard Bible, 1995

THE FRUIT OF THE SPIRIT—NOT "HOW," BUT "IF"

Over the generations, there has been a great deal of debate about the Holy Spirit. The debate is all over the place. From, "Is the Spirit deity and should he be worshipped?" to "How does the Spirit dwell in an individual?" We'll leave those voluminous debates to another venue geared for them.

Our purpose is to investigate and share the aspects of ministry that lead to effectiveness. So rather than stick our toes into those questions, we want to pose a more important question: Is there evidence in your ministry of the Spirit?

We can debate all day on the how, but what about the WHAT? **Is there evidence in your ministry that the fruit born of the**

Spirit is growing in your life? Can we find love, joy, peace, patience, kindness, goodness, faithfulness, gentleness, and self-control in your work? Do we see it in the fruit you are bearing? Do we see it growing in the congregation you are working with? We can grow a church in size and influence without the Spirit being involved, but when we do, the growth will be vain.

Here's a novel idea. As you plan your work, your themes, your programs, and your calendar, ask: "What part of the fruit of the Spirit will this grow in me and my people?"

Do you treat others you are ministering to as clients or as people to be loved? Do you do your work with joy or with a hard edge underscoring some agenda? Does peace follow your work or is it rife with drama? Can you be patient with those you minister to or do you quit on difficult people? How about patience with your elders? Are you a kind individual or are your words launched like missiles? Does faithfulness exude from your work or do you chase after every wind of doctrine that blows through? If we polled the congregation would they characterize you as gentle? In your personal life do you manage your own passions? —*jj*

But you must keep a clear head in everything. Endure suffering. Do the work of a missionary. Devote yourself completely to your work.

2 Timothy 4:5

God's Word Translation

PREACH JESUS

When Paul came to the city of Corinth, he told them that he did not come with excellency of speech (2 Corinthians 2:2). He may not have been a great orator. Maybe if he was alive today he wouldn't have been invited to keynote a special event. But what he did was much more valuable, helpful, and important than being a master communicator. He said in this text, "But I came to know Jesus and Him crucified!" As our old professor, brother Dowell Flatt was known to say, "Boys, that's not about it, that's not nearly it, that is it!!"

Perhaps as much as any time in recent generations, our world desperately needs to hear about Jesus and Him crucified. There are some things we could preach that would be wrong, but when we preach Jesus, we are never wrong. Our world is in desperate need of Jesus. **Jesus really is the answer to every**

struggle in our lives and every problem in our world.

Preaching Christ will not only fill the needs of those who hear us, but will feed the heart and soul of the preacher. The more we study about Christ, and the more we preach Christ, the more we will become like Him. Preaching Jesus brings balance to our life and our preaching.

When we are hurting, we should preach Jesus. When we are weak, we should preach Jesus. When we feel alone, we should preach Jesus. When we feel like our world is imploding, we should preach Jesus. When the church is arguing, we should preach Jesus. When we feel like we are ready to quit, we should preach Jesus.

Jesus is our only hope, He is our salvation, He is our Lord & Master. When we preach Jesus, people will be happy and fulfilled. May God help us to take pleasure in Him as we preach Jesus! —*jj*

But be thou sober in all things, suffer hardship, do the work of an evangelist, fulfill thy ministry.

2 Timothy 4:5

American Standard Version, 1901

NEVER GIVE UP ON PEOPLE

This little book is about being effective and about keys to that end. If you allow it, ministry can make you calloused. You'll be disappointed. You will be let down. You will be lied to and about. And it can wear you down. You can begin to see the worst in people. A handful of people, never in the majority, can get in your head. Others around you will experience it too. Sometimes other ministers, even elders will doubt if people can change. You'll hear: "They will never change." They will pull Jeremiah 13:23 out of its context and cry, "even the Bible says a leopard cannot change its spots." They will tell you that if you take a chance on a person who has failed (which by the way, is everyone) you will get burned.

If you are to be effective you must learn to ignore those voices. Here's the key: **Never**

give up on people! When you feel yourself becoming jaded and hard toward others, remember them as souls—souls who Jesus died for.

Those around you will tell you that they will never change. They will assure you that their motives are impure. Remember, we preach because we DO believe people can change. That is why we are in ministry in the first place. We believe God has the power and the gospel is the power to change them.

Remember further that you cannot read hearts, so stop listening to those who think they can.

That change you are praying so fervently for and working so diligently toward may be one day away from beginning. If you give up on them, you are just the next person in a long line of others who have already given up on them. Be the one who doesn't.

God is the God of second chances. Aren't you glad He is? Aren't you glad He didn't and hasn't given up on you? When He gives up on you, you can start giving up on others. —*dj*

But as for you, exercise self-control in everything, endure hardship, do the work of an evangelist, fulfill your ministry.

2 Timothy 4:5

Christian Standard Bible

THE HIDDEN SECRET OF CONFLICT RESOLUTION

In her cell phone were the personal numbers of Kissenger, Carter, George H.W. Bush, and Israeli leader Menachem Begin. She personally knew four presidents. She had spent her life in high-level Middle Eastern negotiations. And she was talking to me about how to be a great negotiator.

One statement stood out as if in all caps:

"The single most important element in any negotiation is that you go in with a happy, positive outlook. Your odds of success will be significantly increased if you project happiness."

I asked that she repeat that and she did. I smiled and wrote it down and knew, if she was right, that I had this thing called negotiation nailed.

Over time I have found that what she said about that is most often true in ministry. Here's the key: **Your outlook and attitude toward ministry, those you minister to, those you minister with, your elders, and conflict itself affect your effectiveness.**

Go in as a sourpuss, as a negative Nellie (sorry Nellie, I didn't invent the phrase), with a glum outlook, then expecting the worst will become a self-fulfilling prophecy. If you expect the worst you'll get it.

And God is the ultimate optimist. He died for you when you were "yet" a sinner (Romans 5:8), He believed in you when you were an "enemy"(5:10). He invested in you when you were at your darkest and alienated from Him (Ephesians 2:1-3). The Spirit moved Paul to write about this optimism, "And I am sure of this, that He who began a good work in you will bring it to completion at the day of Jesus Christ" (Philippians 1:6).

Furthermore, His Word promises that the way you think will press you toward an outcome (Proverbs 23:7).

So, get happy! I know there's a difference between happiness and joy, but not as big a one as those who like to be miserable and point that out think there is. And, "if you're happy and you know it" don't clap your hands, tell your face.

The outlook you have about your work will affect the effectiveness of your work. Our touchstone verse for this book, 2 Timothy 4:5, in the DJV (Dale Jenkins Version), is paraphrased "make your ministry full of moments of overflowing joy." By the way, don't buy that version, you'd be very disappointed. *—dj*

But you be watchful in all things, endure afflictions, do the work of an evangelist, fulfill your ministry.

2 Timothy 4:5

New King James Version

HARD WORK

Recently I was on a trip with a large number of Senior Christians and while we were riding on a bus to our next stop, I was working on this chapter. The sweet sister across the aisle from me said something about seeing me writing and said, "What are you working on today?" I told her we were putting together a book about effective ministry. After a couple of minutes, she leaned over and said, "We had a preacher one time and we are pretty sure he didn't like us?" Her response was that the preacher didn't really do much other than preach the sermon. She said,"He never hangs around after worship to talk to us, and he typically stays in his office all week and studies."

Brothers, I know that there are sometimes extenuating circumstances that might cause a preacher to leave quickly following the worship, but under normal conditions this should not be the case. I heard a preacher say one time, I don't really care much for people. We certainly don't mean to be ugly about this, but if your attitude is that you don't care much for people and you don't really want to do much other than prepare and deliver a sermon, please, for the sake of the Kingdom and other preachers, find another vocation.

For years people have joked about preachers only working one day a week. To be honest, it is offensive. Or, it would be, if it did not ring so true in the lives of many ministers. If all you want to do is be a public speaker and if you don't want to work hard, please find something else to do. Our brother Paul, told a young preacher that he should preach the Word and fulfill his ministry. We love the preaching the Word part, but we must also learn to love fulfilling our ministry. That means we should stay busy. It means we should fill our lives full of ministry.

Ministry is service to and for others. Our Master worked hard and He taught us by His example that we should be involved in the lives of others. **May God help us to work hard and to love our work.** —*jj*

But you should keep a clear mind in every situation. Don't be afraid of suffering for the Lord. Work at telling others the Good News, and fully carry out the ministry God has given you.

2 Timothy 4:5

New Living Translation

BELIEVING YOU GOT THE BEST END OF THE DEAL

This marriage principle, like many, works in ministry. I wish I could remember who I first heard it from, but it goes something like this. The secret to a thriving marriage is always believing you got the better end of the deal. As long as you feel that you "outkicked your coverage," are fortunate that she accepted your proposal, married up, are more blessed to have her in your life than she isyou, you'll do well. But if that ever changes you will grow frustrated, short with her, feeling like you could have done better, and maybe you'll even begin to wander. It could lead to sin. It could make your marriage weak. It could lead to divorce. As long as both parties in a marriage feel they got the better end of the deal, things can be very healthy (I know, I feel that way every day).

And, it seems to me this same principle holds true with the relationship between a congregation and the minister. Here's the key: **Always believe you got the better end of the bargain.**

Remember when they first offered and you accepted? Remember those early days when you felt so fortunate to be there? Remember the euphoria of preaching in a new place without the baggage of knowledge? If you can, try to keep the feeling that you got the better end of the deal here. If you can, continue to believe that you are blessed to be there. If you can, keep the feeling that you are the fortunate one to get to preach God's Word in that place. Then your effectiveness will increase. As your love and appreciation grows, you will work harder to be the best you can be for the Lord in that place. If you ever start thinking you are God's gift to them, if you ever believe those who tell you how fortunate they are to have you, and you let that sink in too deep, your effectiveness will go down. Now, hear me clearly, I hope, if you do your work well, people will probably say that to you. Just don't let it germinate.

I hope you hear words of great encouragement often and I hope you always feel like you got the better end of the bargain! —*dj*

As for you, always be sober, endure suffering, do the work of an evangelist, carry out your ministry fully.

2 Timothy 4:5

New Revised Standard Version

WHO'S THE BOSS?

"Obey those who rule over you, and be submissive, for they watch out for your souls, as those who must give account. Let them do so with joy and not with grief, for that would be unprofitable for you" (Hebrews 13:17).

I've heard it more than 100 times typically said by some renegade preacher or some hurt and angry preacher, "I don't work for the elders, I work for God." To which I chuckle, "When God starts signing your paycheck that's true, but until then, at least in one sense you work for the elders." But to be more serious, if you are a part of a local congregation and a Christian, then you are under the authority of the elders. It seems clear that shepherds/elders are a part of God's plan (1 Timothy 3; Titus 1; 1 Peter 5, Hebrews 13) and that every church should have them (Titus 1:5).

The roles of elder and preacher can often become complicated. In most of our congregations the elders are the ones who ultimately hire (and fire if it happens) the preacher but the preacher often, because of exposure and opportunity will have more power than any individual elder. But the collective eldership has authority over the minister.

Whether it should or should not be, the reality is that most often the minister will have more training in leadership, honed communication skills, and often more Biblical training than the elders. A wise eldership would do well to use that to their advantage.

It did not take me long to believe I could help the elders at congregations I worked for . I could write announcements for them, I could put out fires for them, I could make important announcements for them. Looking back I am not sure if this was more about my need to feel important than really helping them or if it was more that I didn't trust they'd do it right. And "right", in this case, equaled my way. At least in my heart, I thought I was helping them.

The reality was I was hindering them. I was keeping them from growing. And I was creating more stress for myself. For if I made the announcement and it didn't go well, I had to defend it. If I answered a member on their behalf without consulting them, I was then responsible for what I laid out as what I believed they would do. And, I had members come to me with problems and issues that deterred me from my work and added burdens that I was not selected or ordained to carry.

One night as I aired the laundry list of frustrations with the elders and situations I "had" to deal with, my wife said six words to me that changed my ministry. And they are a key to effective ministry. They are: **Let the elders be the elders**. I was married to a church systems genius and didn't even know it!

When I am tempted to dip my toe back into their area of authority (and thereby disregard God's plan for his work) I remember those words. I still believe that part of my work is to help these men grow, to call them to accountability when I am the only one with that opportunity, and to give them advice as a "voice in the room."

They are the local authority in the congregation. They will be the ones who remain when I leave. They are the ones who will clean up the mess that I might have made or left. And most importantly, by the authority of God, they are the ones to lead the local church in matters where God has not spoken. The more we let the elders be the elders they are given the chance to grow and to lead well.

I have learned that when I do things God's way my stress level goes down and my effectiveness goes up. —*dj*

You're going to find that there will be times when people will have no stomach for solid teaching, but will fill up on spiritual junk food—catchy opinions that tickle their fancy. They'll turn their backs on truth and chase mirages. But you—keep your eye on what you're doing; accept the hard times along with the good; keep the Message alive; do a thorough job as God's servant.

2 Timothy 4:4-6

The Message

TEAM PLAY

Every minister I know wants to be a part of a team. Read Paul's writings. Over and over you'll see his team: Luke, Silas, Barnabas, Timothy, John Mark, etc. Watch Jesus' ministry: there were the 12, the 3, the women, all part of a team. Every preacher I know seems envious of those who are part of a team. But few ever step back to understand how that happens.

Before we launch into this, remember, no team is perfect. Even one of Jesus' team members betrayed Him and all forsook Him for a time. So, get your rose-colored glasses off and accept that with people there will be glitches and challenges.

The team concept really depends on the eldership's willingness to let you be a part of the team. Some elders will be hesitant about this. You are the preacher. They are the elders. Know your role. Sometimes they will feel this way because they have never seen a valuable team working together. Sometimes it will be because they have been burned in the past. And sometimes it might be that they think it would not be a Biblical manner in which to conduct affairs.

Except for the third of these, you might be the key to helping form a great team. Here's the process. Invite them in on your improvement. Assure them you want to be the best you can be. You do. And we can all improve. Ask them for help in making you better than you are as a minister. Keep at them on this. At least twice a year seek input on your personal improvement. After all, they have a front-row seat to seeing your work week after week and a backstage pass to those who come to them with "areas you might need to improve upon." They also have a vested interest in your improvement. They want the church to do well and the better you do the more it will help the congregation. Invite reviews. And, when they give you a suggestion, take it. Work on that area. Try to get better. This will take humility on your part.

After a while of taking their suggestions, growing, and continually assuring them you want to be the best you can be, at some point add, "and I know you guys want to be the best you can be too. Sometimes I run across things that might be useful for you. Would you mind if I share those with you periodically?" You can't do this in the first year or two, but when they have confidence you are really listening and working to be better, then it will probably be met with approval. Don't flood them with information, but just occasionally send them a useful link or article. Make sure it is not offered as a correction or a criticism. And don't run them down. This will kill the team building you are seeking and it's sinful. Taking a positive approach will build a team spirit.

You might also invite them to breakfast now and then or to your house or to some other event away from the building for fun.

If important information is withheld from you, at some point you might discuss with them how your awareness of some of the discussion will make it easier for you to be a proponent of an announcement when it is made. If you will be expected to help in publicizing it and promoting it, it might be useful for you to know the hows and whys of it. Remember, if you are given a place at the table don't abuse it, don't bully, and always respect God's leaders. Also, remember there will always be matters they will need to work on when you are not allowed to be in the room. They are not always discussing you, so stop being so paranoid.

Enjoy the team you have and work toward building it. —*dj*

Stand steady, and don't be afraid of suffering for the Lord. Bring others to Christ. Leave nothing undone that you ought to do.

2 Timothy 4:5

Living Bible

INFLUENCE IS CASH

influence: ˈinflo͞oəns

The word "influence" seems to have fallen on hard times. With people famous for just being famous and people self-styling as "influencers." It had a noble beginning from Old French back in the 14th Century involving the "flowing in" and the "character" of men. In Middle English, its power grew as it became "an outflow of energy that produces an effect."

Sometimes influence flows to you from sources you have little to do with. Coaches, superior athletes, and stars are all in places where a degree of influence is available by the nature of the role. As a minister, you will have a slight automatic degree of influence with some people. But the majority of your influence will come from your life and your work.

Influence provides a microphone. What one does with that microphone will determine if he gets to keep it or reveal if he ever deserved it in the first place.

If you strive to live the life you preach, your influence will increase. If you preach the Word honestly, thoughtfully, preparedly, and faithfully—not plagiarizing, parroting, or pandering—your influence will soar. As people learn to trust that the answers you give them are both Biblical and compassionate your influence will increase. Over time that influence will multiply.

But just because you obtain influence doesn't mean you will keep it. I like to say that **"Influence is cash."** Stay with me. Just as with cash, you cannot spend what you do not have. If you do, you'll be overdrawn.

Sometimes we spend "cash" we don't have. For instance, let's say you want to preach against tobacco use. If you are convicted in this, you should. BUT if you move to

Breckinridge, Kentucky and that is the first sermon you preach, you probably won't last long. You may preach truth clearly, but in all likelihood, you would not yet have the cash/influence you need to preach such a sermon.

But if over time you prove yourself un-radical, not a rabble-rouser, and as one who loves the members there and always preaches the Word, in time you might affect change. Some preachers seem perpetually over-drawn.

The phrase: "They write checks with their mouths that their work can't cover" comes to mind. They don't have the "cash" to affect the change they are proposing. You can't spend what you don't have, you'll get overdrawn.

On the other hand, some preachers seem to be hoarders. They have banked years of solid influence that they are not using. They could speak strongly and gracefully into situations, events, people's lives but don't.

If that is you, I thank you for the life and reputation you have banked, but don't go to heaven with a lot of money left in the account. Use it for the good of souls and to the glory of the Lord.

—dj

But you must keep control of yourself in all circumstances; endure suffering, do the work of a preacher of the Good News, and perform your whole duty as a servant of God.

2 Timothy 4:5

Good News Translation

DON'T LOOK

As we mentioned in a previous key, this one works in marriage too. Sometimes I speak out of both sides of my mouth. I'll say when someone asks me about a congregation that has contacted them and wants to talk to them about moving there: "There's no harm in talking." And, that is true.

Except the way to never have an affair is to never look at other women in any way that might attract you to them. We are humans, and if we look too long we are given to lust or to tarry and end up where we never intended to be. I've never had a Christian man who had an affair tell me he planned on having one.

So, don't look. Don't turn your eye to another woman.

And.

If you love your congregation and want to stay and affect her future and help those people to heaven with you, don't look!

The grass always looks greener from a distance. The larger church, the higher salary, the "better leaders," the more opportunities. Most preachers can always find something attractive somewhere else if they look too long. They will find a place that is more attractive than where they are.

So, don't look. As soon as you do you are sunk. I can't tell you the number of guys who were happy in their work and got a call and DID NOT take it, but the looking led them to looking MORE and to moving within a year.

Dad, Jeff, and I were doing a men's conference together near North Pole, Alaska. Yes, it does exist and Santa Claus is in the phone book! One day, looking for something to do before trying to see the Northern Lights (a real disappointment if you are colorblind) we were driving the Alaska Pipeline. It gave us a long time to talk.

I asked dad, who at that time had been at Roebuck Parkway Church of Christ as the preacher for over 25 years, "Dad, how do you stay at one place for 25+ years?" (* He eventually would die there after 43 years preaching for that good church.)Now, understand our dad was a man of few words and of great humility. He was quiet for a long time. I wish I knew what all went through his mind. We thought he hadn't heard me. Finally, he said, as we waited for great words of wisdom, are you ready?

"You don't move." That was it. That was all. And, now, I know he was right.

He'd had plenty of offers to move. He'd had more than his share of hard days. Over one horrid stretch, they'd lost over 200 members to other congregations. He'd had challenging days with his elders. But he didn't move. He stayed. He rode out the storm. He made amends when he made mistakes. He didn't burn bridges. He loved the people and preached the Word. And he stayed.

Some preachers are into ladder climbing. Note: Not every preacher who moves is. Some need more money. Some have to leave for other reasons. But if you want to do an effective work, don't move. Stay. Determine you are going to do great work in one place.

It's not too great a jump to point out Nehemiah's response to Sanballat and Geshem: "I sent messengers to them, saying, "I am doing a great work and I cannot come down" (Nehemiah 6:2-3). *—dj*

But you must stay calm and be willing to suffer. You must work hard to tell the good news and to do your job well.

2 Timothy 4:5

Contemporary English Version

PEACE

"Can't we all just get along, and love one another?" It seems like everyone is fighting. People argue with their spouses, with their children, at work, and even at church. Political parties, nations, churches, corporations, and even families fight. But, nobody really loves fighting. Some may claim they like it, or act like they enjoy it, but everybody is really searching for peace. And, whether we are willing to admit it or not, we most long for peace in our hearts and minds.

What we learn in time is that there is no true peace without God. At least one reason for this is the fact that we are created in God's image. (Genesis 1:26). In addition to this wonderful news, it is further true that when He created us, He set eternity in each of our hearts (Ecclesiastes 3:11). Because God created us in His image and because He set eternity in our hearts, there will always be a longing and desire to obtain peace. Many people around the world feel a void, and an emptiness, and they will seek to fill that longing with whatever they can find. When God is missing, people will choose to fill that empty void with money, possessions, people, work, and in a multitude of other ways.

However, this void can only be filled with the peace of God. Paul reminded the Philippian Christians and all of God's people that we should "Rejoice in the Lord always; again I will say, rejoice! Let your gentle spirit be known to all people. The Lord is near. Do not be anxious about anything, but in everything by prayer and pleading with thanksgiving let your requests be made known to God. And the peace of God, which surpasses all comprehension, will guard your hearts and minds in Christ Jesus" (Philippians 4:4-7).

—jj

But you should control yourself at all times.
When troubles come, accept them. Do the
work of telling the Good News.
Do all the duties of a servant of God.

2 Timothy 4:5

International Children's Bible

PERSEVERANCE

What I'm about to say is not breaking news, but to watch some minister's actions, you'd think it was. When you signed up for ministry you signed up to sometimes get hurt. There will be times when people will hurt your feelings. There will be people who will be mean to you. There will be times when people will misquote you to harm your work. There will be times when elders will unintentionally hurt you. You will be done wrong. If you can't handle that, go ahead and resign and sell cars or something.

Remember you aren't the first.

Some preached apparently only to add to Paul's bonds (Philippians 1:15-17). Jesus said some would rain persecution on His disciples believing they were doing God a service (John 16:2). Hurt and pain sometimes come with the job.

So, what do you do? You can moan and complain. You can seek to get the person back by being just as mean back to them. You can mentally "unfriend" them. You can tell others what they did to you and try to build a coalition against this horrible person. You can mope around like you lost your best friend. You can move and move and move again.

Or, you can persevere. You can "be steadfast, immovable, always abounding in the work of the Lord, knowing that in the Lord your labor is not in vain" (1 Corinthians 15:58).

Now for the key: **There is a direct correlation between how quickly you get over a hurt and how effective your ministry is.** The longer you hold onto a hurt the more it will hurt. The more you pick at a wound the longer it will take to heal. I have seen it time and again. A guy will get hurt and nurse that wound to the point he loses his effectiveness. He will get discouraged and eventually either let that hurt lead to his dismissal or to moving too soon. But, if you bounce back quickly, if you move forward fast after you've been hurt, you'll just do better. Put it behind you as quickly as you can. Deal with it if you must, but do it and move forward.

"Blessed are you when others revile you and persecute you and utter all kinds of evil against you falsely on my account. Rejoice and be glad, for your reward is great in heaven, for so they persecuted the prophets who were before you" (Matthew 5:11-12)

— *dj*

But as for you, keep your balance in everything! Put up with suffering; do the work of an evangelist; complete the particular task assigned to you.

2 Timothy 4:5

New Testament for Everyone

FAITH—ACTIVE AND REAL

We are a faith people, a people of faith. Our faith is rooted in the Word of God. Founded in the belief that the words of the Bible are more than just words, they are God's Words. Our faith from there grew to our belief in the Word who is the Word (John 1). But—and I know you know this—our faith did not end with our baptism. In fact, when you add water to faith (baptism) the noun of the act becomes the verb of a life!

James painted this picture better than we can when he wrote: "For as the body apart from the spirit is dead, so also faith apart from works is dead." (James 2:26).

We proclaim faith. We use the word often. We admonish others to come to faith and to livc by faith.

But do we?

Do we live by faith? Do we act in faith?

Faith is a little like paint. As long as it is in the can it isn't much. Left in the can long enough a gallon of paint will ruin. Faith left unpracticed and unexercised will too. What are you doing with your faith? With the article "the," "the faith" is that set of beliefs that grow based upon our time in the Word (Romans 10:17). Yet we all know people who have a great knowledge of Bible facts and can parse any doctrine but are not living out the faith they have ingested. So, how are you living your faith out? "We walk by faith, not by sight" (2 Corinthians 5:7).

What are you doing, dreaming of, building? What is there in your life that is evidence that you are living by faith? What are you attempting to do that is not by sight? What are you doing that you would not attempt to do if you did not depend on God to help make it happen? We are not deists.

You can't just talk about faith. To be effective you have to be living it out. So take that paint out of the can and start painting!

Faith involves that belief that God is in control and the future will be better. It's an action that shows we trust in God. Stepping out in Faith gives you such a strength you had no idea you possessed. God is good like that!

Start painting! —*dj*

As for you, always be steady, endure suffering, do the work of an evangelist, fulfil your ministry.

2 Timothy 4:5

Revised Standard Version

WHO'S RIGHT?

My friend James says that if we took all the disclaimers out of our sermons we often wouldn't have much left to say. So I try to avoid them. Yet, this "Key to Effective Ministry" might need one. When I use the word "compromise" below, I am at no point indicating we compromise the Word of God or its teachings. Not only would that not be effective, but it would be sinful. There will be times that you'll have it suggested that if we compromise a belief or Biblical practice we will either grow, attract, or get something done. But don't believe it and give in.

With that out of the way, ministry in the local church is often the art of compromising what you really want and think is best in order to have the influence to do what you do and do it effectively!

Sometimes you have to not get your way and be joyful about it. Sometimes the way you believe is the best way (and it might even be)will not happen, but you have to lose gracefully and move forward happily. If you pout, whine, second-guess, or spread how dumb you think the decision was, you will really lose.

Sometimes when you lose gracefully and work hard for the success of a decision you may not like, you gain credibility and it later pays off.

And, to argue a point of opinion to the point of contention is called a "hobby." And those have often led to division, which is wrong. In a culture that loves to fight over foolishness, we'd do well to learn what is worth investing our influence in and what is not.

Paul told Titus to "avoid foolish controversies, genealogies, dissensions, and quarrels about the law, for they are unprofitable and worthless" (Titus 3:9). And he told Timothy "charge them before God not to quarrel about words, which does no good, but only ruins the hearers (2 Timothy 1:14) and “have nothing to do with foolish, ignorant controversies; you know that they breed quarrels. And the Lord's servant must not be quarrelsome but kind to everyone, able to teach, patiently enduring evil, correcting his opponents with gentleness” (2 Timothy 2:23-25).

Years ago at a marriage seminar I heard Paul Faulkner say: “Don’t invest $100 in a $1 argument.” You can reach a point on a matter of opinion where you are only quarreling over words, which are nothing more than “foolish, ignorant controversies.” To be transparent, I’ve been there. And I’ve won, but ultimately I lost. I lost influence with people. I lost credibility in getting my way.

You possibly do know more about the decision and to strongly contend for what you think best is fine to a point. But there is a point you must compromise and win.

Let me illustrate (that’s when I get in trouble):

There is no Bible verse that tells a preacher what to wear when he preaches if it is within the bounds of modesty. And, you may not like to wear a suit, or a tie, or a jacket, but if wearing a tie gives you an opportunity to preach at a place, why would you not compromise and use that opportunity to teach the Gospel to that audience? Or you may believe there is no such thing as a perfect translation of the Word of God into the English language, and you'd be right, but if a church asks that I use/not use a specific translation, I'd give way for the opportunity to preach God's Word in that place.

You may have very strong emotions about these, but why would you fight to the point you forfeit influence over a matter that is not right or wrong?

Sometimes you must lose to win. —*dj*

But you be sober in all things, suffer hardship, do the work of an evangelist, and fulfill your ministry.

2 Timothy 4:5

World English Bible

THE VOCAL NEGATIVE MINORITY

A preacher once said, "I don't mind being swallowed up by a whale, but I just don't want to be nibbled to death by a thousand minnows!" You've probably noticed that in every church family there is always a small number of people who are negative, bitter, critical, and sometimes they can be ugly. The vast majority of Christians are positive, encouraging, and supportive. As preachers, we sometimes listen more to the minority of voices.

Not that these people shouldn't be heard, but the problem is they often shout the longest and loudest. It might have been brother Ira North who said, "Everyone should have their say, but not everyone will get their way."

What do we do with this small group of people who have convinced themselves that criticism is a spiritual gift? It seems fruitless to spend time arguing with them. Paul talked in rather strict tones to his young preacher friend, Timothy, about these kinds of folk. He stated concisely the issue and he gives us a wise way for it to be handled. "But refuse foolish and ignorant speculations, knowing that they produce quarrels. The Lord's bond-servant must not be quarrelsome, but be kind to all, able to teach, patient when wronged, with gentleness correcting those who are in opposition, if perhaps God may grant them repentance leading to the knowledge of the truth, and they may come to their senses and escape from the snare of the devil, having been held captive by him to do his will"(2 Timothy 2:23-26).

This vocal minority will always be around in every church family. We can and should hear their hearts, but we must not allow them to prevail. Too often preachers and elders allow their voices to get in our heads and not only consume our thinking, but also they cause us to give in or worse, to give up. Let's all pray that they can become convicted and change their hearts and their ways. —*jj*

But as for you, be clear-headed in every situation [stay calm and cool and steady], endure every hardship [without flinching], do the work of an evangelist, fulfill [the duties of] your ministry.

2 Timothy 4:5

Amplified Bible

JUST KEEP GOING

How do you do ministry well? You just keep going. You keep going when your daughter is going through a painful divorce. You keep going when you are depressed. You keep going when you have a conflict with your elders. You keep going when you feel the well is empty. You keep going when your father dies. You keep going when your hero falls. You keep going when there is more month than money. You keep going when you are criticized. You keep going when you struggle with your own faith. You keep going.

There will be a hundred and one million reasons to quit. And you can. At every stage and many months, you will face adversity. But if you want your ministry to impact lives for all of your life, you keep going. You put one ministry step in front of another and you keep going. You grin and bear it and keep going.

"Therefore, since through God's mercy we have this ministry, we do not lose heart...We are hard-pressed on every side, but not crushed; perplexed, but not in despair; persecuted, but not abandoned; struck down, but not destroyed...So then, death is at work in us, but life is at work in you" (2 Corinthians 4:1, 8-10, 12).

There's too much good for you to focus on. There's too much work to be done. There are too many souls to point toward heaven for you to give up.

Just keep going. — *dj*

But you must keep control of yourself in all circumstances. Endure suffering, do the work of a preacher of the good news, and carry out your service fully.

2 Timothy 4:5

Common English Bible

DO SOME THINGS

Someone not in ministry will not understand this. Neither will someone who thinks this work is about keeping the bosses happy. Nor will the person who is just trying to do enough to just get by. This is for the person wanting to "make full proof" of their ministry.

Your work will never end. You'll never get it all done. You'll never find a time when every call has been made, every word study completed, every sermon perfected, every task marked off your to-do list. And if you are not careful everything you do will become work. And your faith will falter. You'll be working a job and not really serving the Lord. My dear friend, Jerry Elder, tells every intern who works with him, "You don't have a job, you have a ministry."

What do you do about it?

Here's the key: **Do some things just because you are a Christian.** Do not tie it to your work, to your pay, instead tie it to your Christianity. You are a Christian but you are also a paid employee of the church. And the responsibilities that fall into your lap as an employee are endless, but your Christianity is NOT a job. Again, there will never be enough time to prepare every message to its best, to visit every shut-in to their satisfaction, to conduct every Bible study you wish to. The end result of all of that may make your work seem fruitless and full of fault. That leaves scant space for simple service to the Savior.

I've found the only relief to this is to do some things that are not "on the clock," not a part of the job description. To do some things that are not on the list of responsibilities and some things that are for your own growth as a member of the true priesthood of every believer.

I can't tell you what that is for you, but I can tell you your soul will be better when you do. For me, it was delivering Thanksgiving bags with my sons each year. We've given out 100 or more and they would all be taken by a family to deliver. I would hold a few back just so I could take them. It was finding small secret gifts or kindnesses I could do without the recipient knowing the source. It was personally supporting a foreign missionary who was under man's radar but doing some great work for God. Here is how it worked for me.

Jesus warned His followers three times in Matthew 6 about doing what they do just to be seen (vss. 2, 5, 16). His divine conclusion was that those who do, already have their reward. I trust it is not your intention to do what you do just to be seen, but I think you see the connection that if all we do is because it is what is expected you'll fall short.

You feed your soul above your public and expected ministry when some of what you do is just between you and the Lord. —*dj*

But be self-controlled in all things, endure afflictions, do the work of an evangelist, and prove your ministry.

2 Timothy 4:5

Modern English Bible

DO SOMETHING

Occasionally, we will hear a preacher say that he has trouble finding enough to do to keep him busy. In our minds that statement seems incredibly difficult to understand. I remember once seeing our Dad mow the grass in his suit and tie because he was so busy in Church work that he didn't have time to change clothes. He was always running from one visit, Bible study, counseling session, or meeting to the next. Some people believe that he worked himself to death.

Now, in full disclosure, it is possible that he overdid it, that he carried his work to an extreme. We are not saying that every preacher needs to or should work as much as he did. However, there is another extreme that we see much more often. It is the preacher who doesn't work very hard at all and is often considered to be lazy. We also know that some preachers do a lot of work that no one else knows about other than the Lord. Please know that this is not directed at you.

We cannot or should not do everything, but we should do SOMETHING. We need to find the right balance for the sake of our marriage, our family, and our personal health. So don't overdo it, but please do SOMETHING.

If you are out of ideas, here are a few starter ideas that you can begin immediately.

(1) Send a personal text to every person on your sick list and let them know that they are in your thoughts and prayers.

(2) Call or text your elders today just to say hello and to see if they need you to pray about anything for them.

(3) Personally reach out to your members who have become unfaithful during the worldwide pandemic and tell them that you miss them. Ask them if there is anything the church can do to help them get back into attending worship.

(4) Make a list of people who you have been thinking about who are not Christians and contact them soon about a Bible study.

Brothers, there is plenty to do. **We can't do it all, but we can all do SOMETHING!** —*jj*

But wake thou, in all things travail thou, do the work of an evangelist, fulfill thy service [fulfill thy service, or office], be thou sober.

2 Timothy 4:5

Wycliffe Bible

LOVE THE PEOPLE, PREACH THE WORD

Our Dad was a man of few words. It wasn't that he didn't know the words or that he thought that words were unimportant. He was a preacher and he preached a lot, but when it came to passing out advice or sharing all of his thoughts, he was very reticent to that. On a trip to Alaska, riding down the Alaskan Pipeline, which he loved, one of us asked, "How do you work with a church for a long period of time without wanting to leave or quit?" After much thought, while we were waiting for a long answer, he finally said, "YOU DON'T MOVE!" Well, that's about it!

When I was about to enter my first full-time work out of college, I went to my Dad's bedroom one night and asked him for his best advice to a young preacher who was just beginning his work. Again, he thought for a long time. Again, I was waiting for some extended, deep theological perspective. He finally said, **"Preach the word and love the people!"** I responded with some smart comment about, "Is that all there is, Is that all you've got?"

After nearly fifty years of preaching, my conviction now is that he was exactly right. These two thoughts sum up the work that preachers do. If we stick to this approach to preaching, we will be successful in God's eyes, and we will bless the lives of all those who know us as well as all those who hear us.

Our brother, Paul, told his young friend, Timothy, "Preach the Word" (2 Timothy 4:1). He added that this is to be done when it's popular and when it's not, in season and out of season. He would also tell Timothy that he needed to fulfill his ministry (vs. 2). That seems to mean stay busy, remain active in your work with God's people. When we love people we will be busy working with them in the service of the Lord.

Probably no one thing you do will make your preaching more effective to the hearers in the local church than to simply love them. The Bible says that if I "have not love, I have become sounding brass or a clanging cymbal" (1 Corinthians 13:1 NKJV). Who wants to be a clanging cymbal, or a noisy brass? May God help us to make sure that our words about Him, match the life we are trying to live for Him. It's still great advice, "Preach the Word & Love the People!" —*jj*

But you, be clear-minded in everything.
Suffer evil. Do the work of an evangelist.
Complete · your ministry.

2 Timothy 4:5

Mounce Reverse Interlinear New Testament

WE ARE ALL THE SAME

It was a tremendous joy recently for us to spend time with more than 250 preachers in Latin America. It was so encouraging to see their passion for preaching, their love for the Lord, their commitment to Kingdom work, and their desire to be pleasing to God.

In each seminar we had a time for the preachers to ask questions about the material we presented as well as any questions about preaching and ministry. In the seminar Sunday night, we answered questions for two hours. If there had been enough time we could have continued for at least two more hours answering the questions they submitted.

The questions they have about preaching and ministry are genuine, thought-provoking, and insightful. It was clear that many of these men of God have the same concerns, challenges, and issues that preachers have in the States.

Their questions were about leadership, about family, about studying the text, about building relationships, and about the stresses of ministry. If there was a topic that we spent more time discussing than other topics it was about how to deal with discouragement, how to handle it when people are critical of our work, and about how to keep going when we feel that ministry has zapped our strength.

That last thought is the one that seems to be a prevailing concern in the life of a majority of preachers we know. How do you keep going, how to keep from quitting when you feel discouraged?

This article is not penned because we have all the answers. We believe that there are some answers and we might reserve the discussion of them for another time. They include the usual suspects; spend more time in prayer, study more, surround yourself with people who encourage, focus more on the joys of ministry, etc. Each of these reasons, and more, deserve much more discussion.

The purpose of this book is to remind us that we are not alone, we are not weird, and we are not necessarily weak, when we deal with these concerns. **Our prayer is that it will help us to remember that we are very much alike.** The fact is these feelings are pervasive around the world. Let's keep turning to Jesus, let's keep praying, and let's keep encouraging one another. We love and appreciate each one of you. We pray that you have a wonderful week in God's Service. We want you to be effective in your work and pledge to you that if you need us, we will do our best to help you and to encourage you. *—jj*

TITLES AVAILABLE FROM TJI

The Living Word: Sermons of Jerry A. Jenkins
Before I Go: Notes from Older Preachers

Thoughts from the Mound (Jeff Jenkins)
More Thoughts from the Mound (Jeff Jenkins)

Beyond the Valley of Death (Jeff Jenkins)

All I Ever Wanted to Do Was Preach (Dale Jenkins)
I Hope You Have to Pinch Yourself (Dale Jenkins)

The Preacher as Counselor (Dale Jenkins and others)

Don't Quit on a Monday (Jeff & Dale Jenkins)
Don't Quit on a Tuesday (Jeff & Dale Jenkins)
Don't Quit on a Wednesday (Jeff & Dale Jenkins)
Don't Quit on a Thursday (Jeff & Dale Jenkins)
Don't Quit on a Friday (Jeff & Dale Jenkins)
Don't Quit on a Saturday (Jeff & Dale Jenkins)

Five Secrets and a Decision (Dale Jenkins)
Centered: Marking Your Map in a Muddled World (Dale Jenkins)
On Moving Well: The Scoop-Meister's Thoughts on Ministry Transitions (Dale Jenkins)
Praying Always: Prayers for Preachers (gift book) (Jeff & Dale Jenkins)
You're Fired! Now What? (Dale Jenkins)

A Minister's Heart (Jeff & Dale Jenkins)
A Youth Minister's Heart (Jeff & Dale Jenkins)
A Mother's Heart (Jeff & Dale Jenkins)
A Father's Heart (Jeff & Dale Jenkins)

*Immerse: A Simple Look at Baptism (*Dale Jenkins)
We Think You'll Love It Here (personalized for guests)

His Word (Daily devos from the New Testament)
His Life (Daily devotionals from Jesus' life & ministry)
My Life (Daily devotionals covering the Christian life)
His Family (Daily devotionals studying the church)

The Glory of Preaching (Jay Lockhart & Clarence DeLoach)
Profiles of Faith & Courage: Interviews with Gospel Preachers (Dennis Gulledge)
Me, You, and the People in the Pews (Tracy Moore)
From Mother's Day to Father's Day (Paul Shero)
Little Fish, Big Splash (Mark Neaves & Shawn Weaver)
The Three Little Ministers (Philip Jenkins)
Choice Over Circumstance (Drake Jenkins)
Pocket Guide for Preachers: 1 Timothy (Joey Sparks & Cole Wade)

Free Evangelism Resources by Jerry Jenkins:
God Speaks Today
Lovingly Leading Men to the Savior

To order, visit ***thejenkinsinstitute.com/shop***

Made in the USA
Monee, IL
26 January 2024